D0710071

Sharing Christ

With Your

Mormon Friends

by

Cary Trivanovich

Promise Publishing Co.   Orange CA 92667

Edited by Margaret Wallace
Technical Assistance by Eleanor Bucher
Cover design by Promise Publishing Co.

Sharing Christ With Your Mormon Friends
Copyright 1991 by Promise Publishing Co.
Published by Promise Publishing Co.
Orange CA 92667

Printed in the United States of America

Trivanovich, Cary
        Sharing Christ With Your Mormon Friends

ISBN 0-939497-22-0

Table of Contents

Introduction

<u>Chapter</u>

Introduction

As a Christian comedian, I meet many pastors and youth workers in my travels throughout the western United States. Whenever I mention my former involvement as a member of the Mormon Church, or my current ministry to Mormons, I hear the same response in every city. I'm told, "This particular area is heavily populated by Mormons—Mormonism is very strong here!" All of these pastors are right in what they say but they are unaware that the same is true of every city throughout the West. The Mormon Church is experiencing phenomenal growth everywhere!

Mormonism began in the early 1800's with only a small group of people but has now grown to over seven million members in the 1990's. All major Christian denominations worldwide recognize it as the largest and fastest growing cult in the United States. Throughout the world today, the Mormon Church is growing at the alarming rate of almost two new members every three minutes—nearly one thousand new members each day. Beautiful Mormon Church buildings are popping up daily in new locations around the world. Forty to fifty thousand full-time missionaries aggressively spread Mormon doctrine door-to-door.

My discussions with pastors have revealed another common issue—most Christians feel inadequate to share Christ with their Mormon friends and relatives. Mormons commonly twist true biblical doctrine and always seem to have an answer to confuse the unprepared Christian. There is a tremendous need for Christians to *be prepared to give an answer*" to their Mormon friends about the reason for their hope in

Christ (I Pet. 3:15). I have written this book in an effort to help meet this need.

Mormons are rarely influenced by tracts (which they call "anti-Mormon literature") or by arguments from strangers (which they call "Mormon-bashing"). I have found that Mormons are most influenced by loving Christian friends who genuinely care for their salvation and patiently share the truth of God's Word over a period of time.

This book was written to be as practical as possible. In the first two chapters, you will gain a clear understanding of what Mormons believe and what the Bible says about reaching them.

In the remaining chapters, we will cover the fundamental issues to discuss in order for your Mormon friends to understand true Christianity. Much of this book is written in script-like form to help you explain God's truth more easily.

It is my prayer that God will work through this book to help you to be more effective in sharing Christ with your Mormon friends.

Chapter One

Why Mormonism
is a Non-Christian Cult

The Mormon Church is officially called The Church of Jesus Christ of Latter-day Saints (LDS). It teaches good moral principles and has excellent social and family activities, yet it is considered to be a "cult" by all major Christian denominations worldwide. Why? Aren't Mormons Christians? Won't they go to heaven when they die? What is so wrong with the LDS Church?

What is a cult?

Modern dictionaries define a cult as an unorthodox religion whose members are devoted to a prominent figure. Therefore, a non-Christian cult is a religious organization which claims to be Christian but denies the essentials of true biblical Christianity. All cults either humanize God, deify man, deny the identity and work of Christ, reject the authority of the Bible or claim new revelation from God. Mormonism does all of these.

In order to share Christ with our Mormon friends effectively, it is important to have a clear understanding of what is wrong with Mormonism in light of the Bible. You may have already heard many of the strange doctrines that Mormonism teaches, such as men becoming Gods or baptism for the dead. Studying all of the unusual doctrines can be time consuming and

Christians may easily become confused while sharing Christ with Mormons

However, there is one doctrine in Mormonism which gives us a "big picture" of its beliefs. Once you understand this doctrine, all of the other doctrines become easy to understand. This big picture in Mormonism is called "Eternal Progression." The doctrine of Eternal Progression forms the structure into which all of the other doctrines fit. It forms the basis of the Latter-day Saints' purpose in life and affects all that they do.

Mormonism's "Eternal Progression"

The doctrine of Eternal Progression claims the following: Eons ago, in the far reaches of the Universe, there lived a God[1] and goddess who bore spirit children. The children were given the opportunity to grow up and become Gods themselves like their parents; but first, the children had to prove themselves worthy. The Gods sent their children through a "probation period" in which they were born into mortal bodies on an earthly planet. Living as mortals, these children had no recollection of their pre-spirit life and were tested by their heavenly father to see if they were worthy to become Gods. Their heavenly father communicated his laws and ordinances to them through earthly prophets. Those mortals who lived good, outstanding lives on their planet and obeyed these laws would be "exalted" to Godhood. Then, as Gods and goddesses, they too would have spirit children who would eventually begin their own progression to Godhood.

1. Mormonism claims actual deity as opposed to idols. To emphasize their claim, a capital G is used for "Gods."

This process has supposedly been going on for "eternities." Simply put, the LDS Church teaches that there are countless Gods. Each God gives birth to more Gods, in an eternal progression of God begetting God.

Mormonism teaches that our God is simply one God within this long line of Gods. It teaches that He began His existence as a spirit person named "Eloheim." Eloheim supposedly lived as a mortal on a distant planet and earned his exaltation to Godhood. He then became God over planet Earth and is now our "heavenly father."

The LDS Church teaches that you and I began our existence as spirit children of this heavenly father and a heavenly mother. We are now going through a probation period on earth. If we accept Mormonism as truth, and if we obey its "gospel laws and ordinances," we, too, will become Gods and goddesses over our own worlds after this life.

The LDS Church explains our part in this progression in their textbook, *Gospel Principles*, pp. 289 and 290:

> "When we lived with our Heavenly Father, he explained a plan for progression to us, his spirit children. We could become like him, an exalted being. The plan required that we be separated from our Heavenly Father and come to earth. This separation was necessary to prove whether we would obey our Father's commandments even though we were no longer in his presence. The plan provided that when earth life was ended, we would be judged and rewarded according to the degree of our obedience.

We would then be assigned the place we
had earned for our eternal home."

The text continues by describing different levels of
heaven, specifically the "celestial kingdom" of heaven
reserved for those who earn "exaltation:"

"WHAT IS EXALTATION? Exaltation is
eternal life, the kind of life that God lives.
He lives in great glory. He is perfect. He
possesses all knowledge and all wisdom.
He is the father of spirit children. He is
a creator. We can become Gods like our
Heavenly Father. This is exaltation. If
we prove faithful and obedient to all the
commandments of the Lord, we will live
in the highest degree of the celestial
kingdom of heaven. We will become exalted, just like our Heavenly Father."

Mormon children learn this in Sunday school:

"AS MAN IS, GOD ONCE WAS; AS GOD IS, MAN MAY
BECOME." That is Eternal Progression.

How Mormons fit Jesus Christ into this picture.

Mormonism teaches that Jesus was the heavenly
father's first spirit child born in the spirit world. They
also teach that God's second spirit child was Lucifer—
Satan himself! That makes God, Jesus, Satan, you and
me all one big family!

According to the Mormons, the heavenly father
chose Jesus to be the savior of mankind—but not a
savior as the Bible presents Him. They teach that
Christ's death and resurrection guarantee all mankind
a resurrection into immortality after this life, regardless of our beliefs about God. After resurrection,

depending on our previous obedience to LDS "gospel law," we may merit Godhood. All those who fall short of complete obedience are not able to become Gods. Instead, they go to a lesser degree of heaven away from the presence of "heavenly father." So, in Mormonism, Jesus Christ provided a two-fold salvation:

1. giving all a resurrected life into immortality, and

2. giving everyone the ability to become Gods, which can be accomplished by obeying LDS "gospel laws and ordinances."

I hope that this big picture of Mormonism's "Eternal Progression" will help you to better understand what your Mormon friends believe. Now, as the old saying goes, **"What's wrong with this picture?"**

Mormonism, with its doctrine of "Eternal Progression," is guilty of false teaching for six major reasons according to the Bible. Like a criminal convicted of six different crimes, each crime in itself being sufficient to condemn him, Mormonism can be classified as a non-Christian cult for any of the following six reasons:

I. Mormonism is a cult because it professes that a plurality of Gods exists.

Mormonism's "Eternal Progression" leads to a belief in countless Gods throughout the universe. In the respected LDS textbook, *Mormon Doctrine*, under the heading, "Plurality of Gods," the claim is made:

> "... there is an infinite number of holy personages, drawn from worlds without number, who have passed on to exaltation and are thus gods."

However, God has made it known to us that He is, and always has been, the only true God:

> "Acknowledge and take to heart this day that the Lord is God in heaven above and on the earth below. There is no other....See now that I myself am He! There is no god besides me" (Deut. 4:39; 32:39).

And again:

> "This is what the LORD says—Israel's King and Redeemer, the LORD Almighty: I am the first and I am the last; apart from me there is no God.... Remember this, fix it in mind, take it to heart, you rebels. Remember the former things, those of long ago; I am God, and there is no other; I am God, and there is none like me" (Isa. 44:6; 46:8-9).

No church can be God's "true church" while professing that other Gods exist. For this reason alone, Mormonism is a non-Christian cult.

II. Mormonism is a cult because it professes that God is an exalted man.

In Mormonism's "Eternal Progression," God is simply a man who once lived on a distant planet and has risen to Godhood. The Mormon "prophet," Joseph Smith, taught that:

> "God himself was once as we are now, and is an exalted man.... I say, if you were to see him today, you would see him like a man in form—like yourselves in all the

person, image, and very form as a man...I am going to tell you how God came to be God. We have imagined and supposed that God was God from all eternity. I will refute that idea.... He was once a man like us" (*History of the Church*, vol. 6, p. 305; also *Mormon Doctrine*, p. 321.)

It is the Bible that Joseph Smith would have to "refute." Numbers 23:19 says that *"God is not a man...nor a son of man."* Also, Psalm 90:2 tells us that God has been God *"from everlasting."*

The God of Mormonism is much smaller than the God of the Bible. The Mormon God is limited—a subordinate and progressive being. Joseph Smith said that God is "like a man in form"—localized in a physical body.

But according to the Bible,

- God is a Spirit (John 4:24);

- He is invisible (I Tim. 1:17); and

- He fills all of Heaven (Jer. 23:24, I Kings 8:27).

The most important foundational doctrine in all of Christianity is knowing the only true God. Jesus said,

> *"Now this is eternal life: that they may know you, the only true God, and Jesus Christ, whom you have sent"* (John 17:3).

Because Mormonism does not accept the true God of the Bible, it is a non-Christian cult.

III. Mormonism is a cult because it professes that men can become Gods.

Because of Mormonism's "Eternal Progression," exaltation to Godhood is the ultimate goal for every Mormon after this life. In *Mormon Doctrine*, p. 321, it is explained:

> "That exaltation which the saints of all ages have so devoutly sought is *godhood* itself ... and you have got to learn how to be gods yourselves, and to be kings and priests to God, the same as all gods have done before you ... To inherit the same power, the same glory and the same exaltation, until you arrive at the station of a god."

Exaltation to Godhood has been a Satanic deception throughout history. The belief that people can evolve into Gods and goddesses is rooted in ancient witchcraft and Gnosticism, as well as in today's "New Age" movement. Satan is getting away with his oldest and most prominent lie through Mormonism as well.

God Himself has proclaimed in His Word:

> *"Before Me no god was formed, nor will there be one after Me"* (Isa.43:10).

Because Godhood is the goal of Mormonism, their claim to be God's "true church" cannot stand as truth.

IV. Mormonism is a cult because it preaches another Jesus.

> *"For if he who comes preaches another Jesus ... such are false apostles"* (II Cor. 11:4, 13 NKJ).

The LDS Church teaches *"another Jesus"* because it teaches a false identity of Jesus Christ. Mormonism denies Christ as the eternal God of the universe. Instead, it holds that He is a literal offspring of God who earned Godhood Himself. The LDS Church has drastically misinterpreted the true identity of Christ. This is evident in the following four LDS teachings about Him:

A. The Mormon Church teaches that Christ had a beginning, born as a spirit child. In *Mormon Doctrine*, p. 281, it is taught:

> "Christ is the Firstborn, meaning that he was the first Spirit Child born to God the Father in pre-existence."

The LDS Church misinterpreted the meaning of "firstborn." The word translated from the original Greek does not even imply birth. Rather, it refers to a position of priority and preeminence over all creation. The Bible confirms that Christ did not have a beginning at all, but was co-existent with the Father *"from everlasting,"* literally "from eternity past" (Micah 5:2, KJV).

B. The Mormon Church teaches that Jesus is the spirit brother of Lucifer (Satan). As explained in their textbooks:

> "Lucifer...this spirit-brother of Jesus" (*Gospel Through the Ages*, p. 15),

"The devil is a spirit son of God who was born in the morning of pre-existence" (*Mormon Doctrine*, p. 192).

According to the Bible, however, Jesus is not the brother of Lucifer—He is the creator of Lucifer!

"For by [Jesus] all things were created that are in heaven and that are on earth, visible and invisible, whether thrones or dominions or principalities or powers. All things were created through Him and for Him." (Col. 1:16, NKJ).

C. The Mormon Church teaches that Jesus was begotten by sexual relations between God the Father and Mary. Again in *Mormon Doctrine*, pp. 546, 547 and 742:

"...our Lord is the only Son of the Father in the flesh.... Christ was begotten by an Immortal Father in the same way that mortal men are begotten by mortal fathers....

"And Christ was born into the world as the literal Son of this Holy Being; he was born in the same personal, real, and literal sense that any mortal son is born to a mortal father. There is nothing figurative about his paternity; he was begotten, conceived and born in the normal and natural course of events, for he is the Son of God, and that designation means what it says."

According to the Bible, Jesus was not conceived by a being "in the flesh." He was conceived by the Holy Spirit and born of Mary **while she was still a virgin:**

"...what is conceived in her is from the Holy Spirit...All this took place to fulfill what the Lord had said through the prophet: 'The virgin will be with child and will give birth to a son..." (Matt. 1:20-23).

D. The Mormon Church teaches that the blood of Christ is unable to atone for some sins:

"Joseph Smith taught that there were certain sins so grievous that man may commit, that they will place the transgressors beyond the power of the atonement of Christ. If these offenses are committed, then the blood of Christ will not cleanse them from their sins even though they repent. Therefore their only hope is to have their own blood shed to atone, as far as possible, in their behalf" (*Doctrines of Salvation*, Vol. 1, p. 135).

This is not the Jesus of the Bible. The Bible says, *"He entered the Most Holy Place once for all by His own blood, having obtained eternal redemption"* (Heb. 9:12).

His blood was shed—not for most sins, but for **all** sins. *"The blood of Jesus, His Son, purifies us from all sin"* (I John 1:7).

Mormons deny the true identity of Christ and also deny that He provides complete salvation for us. The Bible says that false teachers who deny the Lord Jesus are following *"destructive heresies ... bringing swift destruction on themselves"* (II Pet. 2:1). Jude wrote that those who deny Jesus Christ are marked for *"condemnation."*

Jesus said:

> "Whoever believes in Him is not con-
> demned, but whoever does not believe
> stands condemned already because he
> has not believed in the name of God's one
> and only Son" (John 3:18).

> "I told you that you would die in your
> sins; if you do not believe that I am the one
> I claim to be, you will indeed die in your
> sins" (John 8:24).

The LDS belief about the true identity of Jesus
Christ really does matter. It matters for eternity! Only
those who believe in the true Jesus Christ can be Christians.   Our Mormon friends really are in a cult.

V. Mormonism is a cult because it preaches another gospel.

> "But even if we or an angel from heaven
> should preach a gospel other than the one
> we preached to you, let him be eternally
> condemned" (Gal. 1:8).

This warning by the Apostle Paul is of crucial importance.   According to Paul, anyone who preaches a
gospel other than the one he preached is "eternally condemned." The gospel which Paul preached is defined in
I Corinthians 15:1-6:

> "Now, brothers, I want to remind you of
> the gospel I preached to you, which you
> received and on which you have taken
> your stand. By this gospel you are saved,
> if you hold firmly to the word I preached
> to you. Otherwise, you have believed in
> vain. For what I received I passed on to

*you as of first importance: that Christ died
for our sins according to the Scriptures,
that He was buried, that He was raised
on the third day according to the Scriptures, and that he appeared to Peter, and
then to the Twelve. After that, He appeared to more than five hundred...."*

The word *"gospel"* means good news. Paul
describes this good news as the means of our salvation
and explains it in four parts:

- **First**, Christ died for our sins as foretold in the
  Old Testament Scriptures (Isa. 53:5-12).

- **Second**, He was buried, which confirms His
  death.

- **Third**, He rose from the grave on the third day
  as foretold in Scripture (Psalm 16:10, Mark
  9:31).

- **Fourth**, He was seen by eyewitnesses, which
  confirms the truth of His resurrection.

All of the "gospel" accounts (written by Matthew,
Mark, Luke and John) tell the story of this good news.

The LDS gospel, on the other hand, is completely different. As defined in *Mormon Doctrine*, pp. 331-334:

"The gospel of Jesus Christ is the plan
of salvation. It embraces all of the laws,
principles, doctrines, rites, ordinances,
acts, powers, authorities, and keys
necessary to save and exalt men in the
highest heaven hereafter... It is found
only in The Church of Jesus Christ of Latter-day Saints."

The gospel according to Mormonism is the works which men must do to be "exalted" to Godhood. Mormonism does teach that Christ died, was buried and rose again, but only as events which lead to a gospel of obedience to laws:

> "We believe that through the Atonement of Christ, all mankind may be saved, by obedience to the laws and ordinances of the Gospel" (LDS third Article of Faith).

Therefore, Mormonism is preaching a gospel other than what was preached by Paul and the other apostles, just as Paul warned in Galatians 1:8 and repeated in verse 9:

> *"As we have already said, so now I say again: If anybody is preaching to you a gospel other than what you accepted, let him be eternally condemned!"*

We cannot begin with a false gospel and arrive at a true salvation. For this reason alone, Mormonism is not Christian—it is a cult.

VI. *Mormonism is a cult because it is led by false prophets.*

Mormonism began in the early 1800's when fifteen-year-old Joseph Smith, Jr. claimed that God the Father and Jesus Christ came to him in bodily form. Smith claimed that they told him not to join any Christian churches because "they were all wrong," as he put it, and "that all their creeds were an abomination in his sight; that those professors were all corrupt." Smith, claiming to be a prophet of God, founded Mormonism. He presented revelations and scriptures which he said were from God. These scriptures include *The Book of Mormon* (which is supposedly "another testament of Jesus Christ"), *Doctrine and Covenants* and *Pearl of Great Price.*

From Smith's day to the present, Mormons have been led by living "prophets" in what is now known as The Church of Jesus Christ of Latter-day Saints.

Because Joseph Smith claimed to be a prophet of God and introduced Mormonism to the world, he stands as the foundation of the LDS Church. For this reason, it is imperative that we examine his validity as a true prophet of God. I agree with a statement made by one of the later prophets of Mormonism, Joseph Fielding Smith, who said:

> "Mormonism, as it is called, must stand or fall on the story of Joseph Smith. He was either a prophet of God, divinely called, properly appointed and commissioned, or he was one of the biggest frauds this world has ever seen. There is no middle ground.
>
> "If Joseph Smith was a deceiver, who wilfully attempted to mislead the people, then he should be exposed; his claims should be refuted, and his doctrines shown to be false, for the doctrines of an impostor cannot be made to harmonize in all particulars with divine truth. If his claims and declarations were built upon fraud and deceit, there would appear many errors and contradictions, which would be easy to detect. The doctrines of false teachers will not stand the test when tried by the accepted standards of

measurement, the scriptures" (*Doctrines of Salvation*, Vol. 1, p. 188).

"Many errors and contradictions" is an understatement. Joseph Smith has contradicted the Bible with his teaching of a plurality of Gods, a false doctrine of the identity of Jesus Christ and the preaching of another gospel. These things classify him as a false prophet (II Cor. 11:4,13). But he was also a false prophet because he gave false prophecies! According to the Bible, anyone who claims to be a prophet of God but whose prophecies fail to happen is a false prophet. Deuteronomy 18:21-22 gives us this biblical test for a true prophet:

> "You may say to yourselves, 'How can we know when a message has not been spoken by the LORD?' If what a prophet proclaims in the name of the LORD does not take place or come true, that is a message the LORD has not spoken. That prophet has spoken presumptuously. Do not be afraid of him."

Also in Jeremiah 23:32:

> "Indeed, I am against those who prophesy false dreams,' declares the LORD. 'They tell them and lead my people astray with their reckless lies, yet I did not send or appoint them. They do not benefit these people in the least,' declares the LORD."

A prophet of God has never, and can never, prophesy falsely. Yet Joseph Smith made an overwhelming number of false prophecies which are still recorded in LDS "scriptures" and historical writings. (See Chapter Six: Exposing Joseph Smith as a False Prophet.)

All of Mormonism rests on the validity of Joseph Smith as a prophet of God. Jesus said:

> *"Beware of false prophets ... by their fruits you will know them"* (Matt. 7:15-20 NKJ).

By the fruits of the "prophet," Joseph Smith, we know that Mormonism is a non-Christian cult.

Chapter Two

What the Bible Says About Sharing Christ With Mormons

The religion of "Mormonism" itself is not mentioned in the Bible—not directly, that is. However, Mormons are latter day false prophets and false teachers which the Bible warns would be among us:

> "But there were also false prophets among the people, just as there will be false teachers among you. They will secretly introduce destructive heresies, even denying the sovereign Lord who bought them - bringing swift destruction on themselves. Many will follow their shameful ways and will bring the way of truth into disrepute. In their greed these teachers will exploit you with stories they have made up..." (II Pet. 2:1-3).

> "For the time will come when men will not put up with sound doctrine. Instead, to suit their own desires, they will gather around them a great number of teachers to say what their itching ears want to hear. They will turn their ears away from the truth and turn aside to myths" (II Tim. 4:3-4).

Like the *"false teachers"* in biblical times, Mormons *"oppose the truth... who, as far as the faith is concerned, are rejected"* (II Tim. 3:8). LDS leaders are like the false teachers who *"want to be teachers of the law, but they*

*do not know what they are talking about or what they
so confidently affirm"* (I Tim. 1:7).

In Bible passages such as these, God gives us instructions about how to share Christ with our Mormon friends. To prepare us for this process, the Bible provides all we need—a foundation, a method and a message.

OUR FOUNDATION

> *"But you, dear friends, build yourselves
> up in your most holy faith and pray in the
> Holy Spirit"* (Jude 20).

Jude wrote this exhortation to Christians in his epistle which is devoted entirely to the subject of false teachers. He gave us two foundational principles, often taught throughout scripture, which are crucial when dealing with false teachers.

1."Build yourselves up in your most holy faith."

Knowing God is a crucial foundation when dealing with false teachers. God communicates clearly that He desires for us to be built up in Him. This must be the initial step in sharing Christ with our Mormon friends. Paul says:

> *"I tell you this so that no one may deceive
> you by fine-sounding arguments ... So
> then, just as you received Christ Jesus as
> Lord, continue to live in Him, rooted and
> built up in Him, strengthened in the faith
> as you were taught, and overflowing with
> thankfulness. See to it that no one takes
> you captive through hollow and deceptive
> philosophy..."* (Col. 2:4, 6-8).

More than anything God wants us to focus on Him—
to know and to worship Him. Knowing God and being
built up in our faith requires becoming rooted in God's
Word. The Bible is powerful, indispensable and brings
a life-changing relationship with the Lord. I can certainly testify to that. Shortly after coming to Christ and
leaving Mormonism, I began searching through the
Bible for truth to share with my Mormon friends. I soon
became absorbed in reading God's truth. The result of
so much time in God's word was growth—not only in
knowledge, but in an increasing love for Him. I became
more firmly *"rooted and built up in Him."*

If our daily lives are grounded on and built up in
Christ, our Mormon friends will notice our God-given
courage—just as Peter and John's accusers saw their
courage and, realizing *"that they were unschooled, ordinary men, [the accusers] were astonished and they
took note that these men had been with Jesus"* (Acts
4:13).

2. *"...and pray in the Holy Spirit."*

Prayer is the other foundational principle which
Jude gave us for dealing with false teachers. Our
strongest weapon to combat the deception of Mormonism is prayer. I always say, "If we leave God out,
we don't have a prayer!"

Paul reminds us:

> *"For our struggle is not against flesh and
> blood, but against the rulers, against the
> authorities, against the powers of this
> dark world and against the spiritual
> forces of evil in the heavenly realms"* (Eph.
> 6:12).

Because our struggle is against evil forces, Paul exhorts us to stand firm in the Lord and also *"with this in mind, be alert and always keep on praying"* (vs. 18).

Our LDS friends are not intentionally following false doctrine. They are deceived! It is *"the spiritual forces of evil"* which are working in their hearts. I believe that the biblical warnings about *"another gospel"* and *"another Jesus"* were given because we need to be aware of Satan's incredible ability to deceive. Romans 1:16 states that the gospel of Christ *"is the power of God for the salvation of everyone who believes."* Since the true gospel of the true Christ is the only means of salvation, it must be Satan's number one goal to keep people from true understanding of that gospel. Mormonism's counterfeit gospel is *"the trap of the devil, who has taken them captive to do his will"* (II Tim. 2:26).

This deception which they are experiencing is powerful and bypasses their intellectual reasoning about spiritual truth. I know many Mormons who are very intelligent, educated people; however, when it comes to spiritual issues, it seems as though their intellect is switched off. We could share convincing arguments with Mormons for hours, present evidence of fraud in LDS scripture or even clearly expose false prophecies from Joseph Smith, but find that none of these issues persuade them. Mormons turn their backs on the facts. Instead of searching God's Word for themselves, they trust in a "testimony" instilled by their leaders claiming that Mormonism is God's "true church." For this reason, we are absolutely powerless to change their minds by our own convincing arguments.

There is good news for us, though. It is the Holy Spirit's role to convict our friends' hearts, not our role.

Jesus said it is the Holy Spirit who *"will convict the world of sin"* (John 16:8 NKJ). We can plant the seeds, but it is *"God, who makes things grow"* (I Cor. 3:7). We need only to recognize this and place our trust in God for His work in their hearts.

I believe that the more we admit our dependence upon the Lord and are on our knees in prayer, the more power we will see in our witness. The moment we begin to rely on our own ability to persuade our Mormon friends, we will undercut God and hinder His working through us. Satan does not care how much you try to convince your Mormon friends because as long as he has you away from prayer, he is intervening. We need God!

When we fully comprehend the importance of prayer that relies upon God to convict hearts, we can speak to Mormons with full confidence, knowing that God is in control! As we share Christ with them, we never need to feel frustrated or defeated, as if we might "blow it" by our choice of words. If God, in His sovereign will, chooses to *"grant them repentance"* (II Tim. 2:25) and bring them to Himself, He will get the job done perfectly regardless of our imperfections. Since I grasped this most important foundation of prayer with reliance upon God, I have had the joy of confidently sharing Christ with Mormons and watching the power of God work in them for salvation.

> *"Commit your way to the LORD; trust in Him and He will do this: He will make your righteousness shine like the dawn, the justice of your cause like the noonday sun"* (Psalm 37:5-6).

OUR METHOD

> *"Preach the Word; be prepared in season
> and out of season; correct, rebuke and en-
> courage - with great patience and careful
> instruction"* (II Timothy 4:2).

Our method of sharing Christ with those who *"turn
their ears away from the truth and turn aside to myths"*
(II Tim. 4:4) is found in Paul's letters to Timothy. These
letters are filled with valuable instruction for us as we
witness to our Mormon friends. Let's look at three key
factors about sharing Christ found in the verse above.

1. Use the Bible!

"Preach the Word," Paul wrote. The Bible is our tool:

> *"All Scripture is God-breathed and is
> useful for teaching, rebuking, correcting
> and training in righteousness, so that the
> man of God may be thoroughly equipped
> for every good work"* (II Tim. 3:16-17).

Once while sharing with a Mormon missionary, I
asked him to read a Bible verse to me. As he read it,
his voice and hands trembled. The Word of God had
an effect on him that I'll never forget. Just as Hebrews
4:12 says:

> *"For the Word of God is living and active.
> Sharper than any double-edged sword, it
> penetrates even to dividing soul and spirit,
> joints and marrow; it judges the thoughts
> and attitudes of the heart."*

I would not want to be caught witnessing to a Mormon without my Bible. Without it, I have nothing to say!

2. Be ready!

"Be prepared in season and out of season; correct, rebuke and encourage," Paul goes on to say. As believers, we will meet many Mormons throughout our lives. It is important to study God's truth in order to "correct" Mormon teaching. There's nothing like being ready and confident to share the truth with Mormons at any time and respond to their claims against Christianity.

> *"But in your hearts set apart Christ as Lord. Always be prepared to give an answer to everyone who asks you to give the reason for the hope that you have..."* (I Pet. 3:15).

3. Be loving!

Paul admonishes us to speak *"...with great patience and careful instruction."* How easy it is to end up in an argument with Mormons over what is truth; instead, we should be *"speaking the truth in love"* (Eph. 4:15). Always remember that your attitude will make more of an impact on them than your convincing arguments. Mormons are very sensitive about opposition to their church. It is crucial for them to know that you are genuinely concerned for their salvation. If they sense that you are just out to win a theological debate, they may tune you out and, therefore, never receive the truth. A loving, confident witness with *"great patience and careful instruction"* will win their respect.

Paul wrote these valuable words about sharing with false teachers:

> "Don't have anything to do with foolish and stupid arguments, because you know they produce quarrels. And the Lord's servant must not quarrel; instead, he must be kind to everyone, able to teach, not resentful. Those who oppose him he must gently instruct, in the hope that God will grant them repentance leading them to a knowledge of the truth, and that they will come to their senses and escape from the trap of the devil, who has taken them captive to do his will" (II Tim. 2:23-26).

OUR MESSAGE

> "For I resolved to know nothing while I was with you except Jesus Christ and Him crucified" (I Corinthians 2:2).

Our message to Mormons is the same as to any unbeliever separated from God for eternity. Our message is Jesus Christ! Since our goal is their salvation, then there is no other message because "salvation is found in no one else, for there is no other name under heaven given to men by which we must be saved" (Acts 4:12). Our message to Mormons is two-fold—first, Christ's true identity and second, His salvation for us.

Mormons need to comprehend that Christ is God but first they need to come to understand who God really is—the eternal, self-existent, omnipresent, all-powerful, all-knowing, only true and living God. Understanding the true God of the Bible is the foundation for understanding who Christ is, and knowing Him is eternal life!

> *"Now this is eternal life: that they may know you, the only true God, and Jesus Christ, whom you have sent"* (John 17:3).

By sharing with our Mormon friends what the Bible says about the only true, eternal God, we can expose their foundational doctrine of "Eternal Progression" as false. Once we have established the biblical truth about God, we can direct them toward understanding the true identity of Christ and their need for Him.

YOUR PRESENTATION

In the following chapters, you will find information about important issues to discuss with a Mormon friend. I have quoted sound biblical evidence for each issue you want him to consider. I have also listed common Mormon claims regarding these subjects and how to respond to them. Try to share with your friend without outside interruptions or time constraints.

Direct the conversation.

When sharing with your Mormon friend, make it your goal to discuss the doctrine of God and the true identity of Jesus Christ. It is very important to control the direction of the conversation. Usually, when a Mormon cannot respond to your biblical claims, he will bring up a different issue which he feels more comfortable discussing. Do not let him sidetrack you with other issues, such as the priesthood or baptism for the dead. While these are important issues to a Mormon, they will not bring him any closer to knowing Christ. If he attempts to change the subject, patiently listen to him and then promise to address the issue he has raised after you are finished with your point. Have a pencil and paper handy, so that when your friend raises a different issue, you can write it down and promise to discuss it later. Then continue where you left off. By doing this, you can direct the conversation.

Pose questions.

By posing important questions to your Mormon friend, you can direct his thoughts. Normally, when a Christian and a Mormon are debating, both are focusing on their own argument and not really comprehending what the other is saying. However, if you pose a question to your friend, his focus must be on answering your question.

For example, while discussing the eternal existence of God, open your Bible to Psalm 90:2:

> *"From everlasting, to everlasting, thou art God."*

ASK: How long does this say that God has been God? Does the LDS Church teach that God has been God *"from everlasting"*?

By posing questions like these, you can direct your friend's thoughts toward the truth of God's Word.

What to use:

Use the King James Version of the Bible. The LDS Church officially uses the King James Version, believing it to be the most accurate. Therefore, most Mormons will frown on using any other version. For this reason, this version is quoted in Chapters Three through Seven.

Use the *Book of Mormon* and the LDS textbooks— *Gospel Principles* and *Mormon Doctrine.* Your friend may have copies of these. If not, simply read the quotes from this book.

Use this book as a guide: If your relationship with your LDS friend is close enough to allow you to use this book openly as a guide, you will find it very helpful to have the information readily available. However, in some cases, it may be more appropriate to copy notes of your own ahead of time.

Chapter Three

Discussing the Doctrine of God

Be sure your Mormon friend understands exactly what the LDS doctrine of "Eternal Progression" means. Pose these questions:

- Do you know what Mormonism's Eternal Progression is? (Explain as on pp. 2-4.)

- According to Eternal Progression, aren't we God's children in a probation period here on earth, striving to become Gods just like our Heavenly Father? (If necessary, refer to *Gospel Principles*, quoted on p. 4.)

- According to Eternal Progression, wasn't our Heavenly Father once a man who has now risen to Godhood? (If necessary, refer to Joseph Smith quoted on pp. 6-7.)

- Then, according to Eternal Progression, our Heavenly Father was once in subjection to a God over him? (If necessary, quote Joseph Smith:)

   "And where was there ever a father without first being a son? Whenever did a tree or anything spring into existence without a progenitor? And everything comes in this way ... Hence if Jesus had a Father, can we not believe that He had a Father also?" (*Mormon Doctrine*, p. 577; and *Teachings of the Prophet Joseph Smith*, p. 373.)

• If every God must earn Godhood, then who was the first God and where do you suppose he came from? (This is a good question to ask because the LDS Church does not have an official explanation for how Eternal Progression began. At this point, you have set the stage to show him what the Bible says about God.)

SHOW WHAT THE BIBLE SAYS ABOUT GOD

He is the only true God.

> Isaiah 43:10: *"Ye are my witnesses, saith the Lord, and my servant whom I have chosen: that ye may know and believe me, and understand that I am he: before me there was no God formed, neither shall there be after me."*

> Isaiah 44:6: *"Thus saith the LORD the King of Israel, and his redeemer the LORD of hosts; I am the first, and I am the last; and beside me there is no God."*

ASK: If God is the first and the last, then how can Eternal Progression be true?

> Isaiah 44:8: *"...Is there a God beside me? Yea, there is no God; I know not any."*

> Isaiah 45:5: *"I am the LORD, and there is none else, there is no God beside me..."*

> Isaiah 46:8-9: *"Remember this, and shew yourselves men: bring it again to mind, O ye transgressors. Remember the former things of old: for I am God, and there is none else; I am God, and there is none like me."*

Various LDS claims of many Gods:

Your friend may try to debate with you, using any of the following claims. Each time you respond to his claim, remind him that there is only one true God according to the Bible!

CLAIM #1: These verses in Isaiah mean that He is the only God for us to worship.

YOUR RESPONSE: It's true that we should only worship God, but in Isaiah, God is proclaiming that He is the only God Who exists. He says, "...there was no God formed" (43:10), "...there is none like me" (46:9).

CLAIM #2: These verses in Isaiah mean that He is the only God of this Earth.

YOUR RESPONSE: Doesn't the LDS Church claim that our Heavenly Father and Jesus and the Holy Ghost are all separate Gods for this Earth? (Yes.)

Joseph Smith said, "... we have three Gods anyhow, and they are plural; and who can contradict it?" (*Teachings of the Prophet Joseph Smith*, p. 370).

God says that He is not only the one God of this earth, but of all the heavens and all the stars:

> Isaiah 45:12: "*I have made the earth, and created man upon it: I, even my hands, have stretched out the heavens, and all their host [literally "starry host"] have I commanded.*"

> Deuteronomy 10:14: "*Behold, the heaven and the heaven of heavens is the LORD'S thy God, the earth also, with all that therein is.*"

The Bible says He made the heavens, all the stars and constellations:

> Job 9:8-9:   *"Which [God] alone spreadeth out the heavens, and treadeth upon the waves of the sea. Which maketh Arcturus, Orion, and Pleiades, and the chambers of the south."* (Arcturus, Orion, and Pleiades are constellations; see also Job 38:31-33.)

> Nehemiah 9:6:   *"Thou, even thou, art LORD alone; thou hast made heaven, the heaven of heavens, with all their host..."*

CLAIM #3: Isaiah is talking about idol-gods.

YOUR RESPONSE: That is correct. It is because people were worshipping idol-gods that God reaffirms His position as the only true God (Isa. 44:9-20). Therefore, no true God has ever existed before Him or ever will exist after Him (43:10).

CLAIM #4: I Corinthians 8:5 says, *"there be gods many and lords many."*

YOUR RESPONSE: Read this verse in context:

> *"As concerning therefore the eating of those things that are offered in sacrifice unto idols, we know that an idol is nothing in the world, and that there is none other God but one. For though there be that are called gods, whether in heaven or in earth, (as there be gods many, and lords many,) But to us there is but one God, the Father, of whom are all things, and we in him; and one Lord Jesus Christ, by whom are all things, and we by him"* (I Cor. 8:4-6).

This passage discusses idols which were worshipped as Gods, even though there is really only one true God. I Chronicles 16:26 reasserts:

"For all the gods of the people are idols:
but the LORD made the heavens."

CLAIM #5: In John 10:34, Jesus said, *"Ye are gods."*

YOUR RESPONSE: John 10:34 is a quotation of Psalm 82:6 where human judges were called gods, although they were merely men and would *"die like men."* Jesus was not telling these Jewish men that they were actual Gods. Nowhere in the Bible did He indicate that men can become Gods.

CLAIM #6: Genesis 1:26 says, *"And God said, let us make man in our image, after our likeness,"* which means that there is more than one God.

YOUR RESPONSE: The *"us"* and *"our"* refer to the Father, Son and Holy Spirit which indicates the triune nature of God. Notice in this verse and in the following verses that only one God is speaking.

CLAIM #7: These few verses in Isaiah aren't enough to prove your point to me.

YOUR RESPONSE: These verses in Isaiah are only an example of the teaching of the whole Bible. I can show you that the Bible from beginning to end affirms the existence of only one true God, but could you show me just one verse in the Bible to support your belief in many Gods? (Here are other verses affirming only one true God: Deuteronomy 4:35,39; Deuteronomy 32:39; I Samuel 2:2; II Samuel 7:22; I Kings 8:60; I Chronicles 17:20; Psalm 18:31; Mark 12:32; I Corinthians 8:4-6; James 2:19.)

***God has always been God from eternity past;
He is not an exalted man.***

ASK: Doesn't the LDS Church teach that God hasn't always been God, but that He was a man who earned his way to Godhood through Eternal Progression? (Yes.) The Bible says in:

Numbers 23:19: *"God is not a man, that he should lie; neither the son of man..."*

Psalm 90:2: *"From everlasting, to everlasting, thou art God."*

If He has been God *"from everlasting,"* how long has He been God? (Forever past.)

Does Mormonism teach the true eternal nature of God? (No.)

***God is a Spirit who fills all of Heaven;
He is not localized in a physical body.***

He is pure Spirit: John 4:24: *"God is a Spirit..."*

He is invisible: I Timothy 1:17: *"Now unto the King eternal, immortal, invisible, the only wise God..."*

He fills all of Heaven: Jeremiah 23:24: *"Can any hide himself in secret places that I shall not see him? saith the LORD. Do not I fill heaven and earth? saith the LORD."*

I Kings 8:27: *"But will God indeed dwell on the earth? Behold, the heaven and heaven of heavens cannot contain thee; how much less this house that I have builded?"*

Various LDS claims that God has a physical body:

CLAIM #1: God is a man; He has body parts (Mormons quote Bible passages like Exodus 33:11, *"The LORD spake unto Moses face to face..."*).

YOUR RESPONSE: That is figurative language. Psalm 91:4 says, *"He shall cover thee with his feathers, and under his wings shalt thou trust..."* Is God also a bird? No. The Bible often uses figurative language to describe a spiritual reality.

(Note: Exodus 33:11 quoted above cannot be literal. In verse 20, the Lord says, *"Thou canst not see my face: for there shall no man see me, and live."* Also Hebrews 11:27 explains that Moses, by faith, *"endured, as seeing him who is invisible."*)

CLAIM #2: What about the appearances of God in the Old Testament?

YOUR RESPONSE: Those were not appearances of God the Father. He never appeared visibly. The Apostle Paul emphatically stated that no one has ever seen God the Father:

> *"Who only hath immortality, dwelling in the light which no man can approach unto; whom no man hath seen, nor can see ..."* (I Tim. 6:16).

Those Old Testament appearances were "theophanies," or manifestations of God, by the Son who alone declares Him:

> *"No man hath seen God at any time; the only begotten Son, which is in the bosom of the Father, he hath declared him"* (John 1:18).

Review the nature of God in contrast with the God of Mormonism.

GOD OF THE BIBLE:	GOD OF MORMONISM:
*The only true God.	*One among many Gods.
*Has always been God.	*Man risen to Godhood.
*A Spirit who fills all of Heaven.	*A man localized in a physical body.
*A self-existent Supreme Being.	*A subordinate and progressive being.

The God of Mormonism is much smaller than the God of the Bible. The God of the Bible is infinite in ability and knowledge. He spoke the heavens into existence (Gen. 1:1-8; Job 9:8-9; Neh. 9:6) and upholds all things by the word of His power (Heb. 1:3).

Chapter Four

Discussing Jesus Christ and the Trinity

Once you have discussed the doctrine of the one true God of the Bible, you have prepared your friend for a discussion of the true identity of Jesus Christ. This is the most important issue to discuss with him. When he sees what the Bible says about who Jesus Christ really is, he will be at the threshold of accepting the gospel message of salvation.

This chapter discusses both Jesus Christ **and** the Trinity for one important reason: Establishing the true identity of Jesus Christ usually involves an explanation of the Trinity. Because your LDS friend will appreciate this explanation, you should take the time to examine the biblical evidence and present it to him. I have seen Mormons accept Christ as soon as they understood that He truly is God.

If you have only a few moments to talk with a Mormon, this is the issue to raise. The true identity of Jesus Christ is the central factor of our salvation. It is the most powerful argument when confronting Mormonism, and thus, a very effective approach to use when your time is limited.

Be sure your Mormon friend understands what the LDS Church teaches about the identity of Christ.

It teaches that Christ had a beginning, born as a spirit-child.

Mormon Doctrine, p. 281 says, "Christ is the Firstborn, meaning that he was the first Spirit Child born to God the Father in pre-existence."

It teaches that Christ is the brother of Lucifer (Satan).

Gospel Through the Ages, p. 15 says, "'Lucifer ... this spirit-brother of Jesus."

Mormon Doctrine, p. 192 says, "The devil is a spirit son of God who was born in the morning of pre-existence."

SHOW THE TRUE IDENTITY OF JESUS CHRIST

Christ is not the brother of Lucifer—
He is the Creator of Lucifer!

Colossians 1:16 says,

> *"For by him were all things created, that are in heaven, and that are in earth, visible and invisible, whether they be thrones, or dominions, or principalities, or powers: all things were created by him, and for him."*

(NOTE: *"Principalities and powers"* refers to the devil (Lucifer)—Ephesians 6:11-12. Also, the Bible confirms that Lucifer is a created being—Ezekiel 28:13,15.)

Christ has existed from eternity past; He was not born to God the Father in pre-existence.

Micah 5:2, in reference to the coming birth of the Messiah, says:

"But thou, Bethlehem Ephratah, though thou be little among the thousands of Judah, yet out of thee shall he come forth unto me that is to be ruler in Israel; whose goings forth have been from of old, from everlasting."

(NOTE: *"From everlasting"* in the Hebrew text literally means *"from eternity."* Jesus Christ has existed from eternity!)

Jesus Christ is the one eternal God who became flesh.

John 1:1-3, 14 says,

"In the beginning was the Word, and the Word was with God, and the Word was God. The same was in the beginning with God. All things were made by him; and without him was not any thing made that was made .... And the Word was made flesh, and dwelt among us, (and we beheld his glory, the glory as of the only begotten of the Father,) full of grace and truth."

I Timothy 3:16: *"And without controversy great is the mystery of godliness: God was manifest in the flesh..."*

EXLAIN THE TRINITY

Sometime during your discussion about the identity of Christ, your friend will probably ask you to explain how Jesus can be God since He prayed to God. Mormons think Christians believe that Jesus is the Father.

Frequently a Mormon will ask, "Did Jesus pray to Himself in the Garden of Gethsemane?" or "Was Jesus a ventriloquist when a voice from heaven said, 'Thou art my beloved Son, in thee I am well pleased'"? The answer will be clear when the Trinity is understood.

The concept of the Trinity is not something we easily relate to in our limited, three-dimensional thinking. Understanding how great God truly is in contrast with the LDS concept of God (as Chapter Three explains) will help in comprehending what the Bible says about His triune nature. Also, we must be willing to submit in faith to what God's Word says concerning this doctrine.

Define what Christians mean by "Trinity."

Within the nature of the one true God, there are three separate persons; the Father, the Son and the Holy Spirit, and these three persons eternally co-exist as the one God.

FATHER — IS NOT — SON — IS NOT — HOLY SPIRIT — IS — GOD — IS — IS

Tri-unity is perhaps a better word to describe the three-fold nature of God.

It is important to understand that Christians do not believe that Jesus is God the Father. Rather, He is the **second** person of the triune God; that is why He could communicate with the Father.

Biblical evidence for the Trinity.

1. The Bible affirms that there is only one true God (Deut. 4:35,39; 32:39; Isa. 44:6,8; 45:5, James 2:19).

2. The Father, Son and Holy Spirit are each called God in the Bible.

- The Father is called God (John 6:27; Phil. 2:11).

- Jesus is called God (John 1:1, 14; Titus 2:13, Hebrews 1:8; I John 5:20).

- The Holy Spirit is called God (Acts 5:3-4; also compare I Cor. 3:16 with 6:19).

3. The Father, Son and Holy Spirit are named as one. Matthew 28:19 says, *"in the name of the Father, and of the Son, and of the Holy Ghost."* Notice that it says *"name,"* not *"names."* In the original Greek, the three are united into one singular name. Literally, it means *"in the One Whose name is Father-Son-Holy Ghost."*

4. Jesus claimed to be the same God in union with God the Father. In John 10:30, Jesus said, *"I and my Father are one."* This does not mean one only in purpose, as Mormons claim. The Jews attempted to stone Jesus when He made this statement. Would they have wanted to stone Him for being one in purpose with God? No, they were also one in purpose with God. The Jews knew what Jesus meant.

The Greek text in John 10:30 verifies that Jesus claimed to be God. The Greek word for "one" is neuter in gender and demands the meaning of "one in essence." The Greek text literally shows a distinction of two persons who share the same essence: *"I and my Father, We are one (essence)."*

LDS CLAIM: In John chapter 17, Jesus prays for believers *"that they all may be one."* So, does that mean we are all going to be the same person in heaven?

YOUR RESPONSE: In this chapter, the word "one" in Greek does not refer to one in essence as in John 10:30. Just as the context reads, it refers to one in sanctification and truth.

If Jesus is God, why did He pray to God?

> "Saying, Father, if thou be willing, remove this cup from me: nevertheless not my will, but thine, be done" (Luke 22:42).

This is the one question that Mormons most often ask. To answer it requires a mini Bible study with your friend. The Bible gives a clear explanation when examined in the original Greek. Mormons (and most Christians) are not aware of this because they do not study the Bible in such depth. Your friend may not even be aware that the New Testament was originally written in the Greek language.

Ask your friend to look at Philippians chapter two with you and then you can show him why Jesus, who is God, prayed to God.

YOUR RESPONSE: Jesus is the second person in the triune nature of God. He "became flesh" (John 1:14). Although He became a man, He was still fully God. In order to redeem us from our sins, He willingly laid aside His divine rights as God and humbled Himself as a man. It was God's perfect plan that God the Son would live on earth as a man and be in subjection to the will of God the Father. This is explained in the Greek text of Philippians 2:6-8. Specific words in the Greek (printed here in bold) give clear meaning to the passage:

> *"Who, being in the **form** of **God**, thought*
> *it not robbery to be equal with God: But*
> ***made** himself **of no reputation,** and took*
> *upon him the form of a servant, and was*
> *made in the likeness of men: And being*
> *found in **fashion** as a man, he humbled*
> *himself, and became obedient **unto***
> ***death,** even the death of the cross."*

Now look at the Greek meaning of these key words and read them in their context:

"Form" *(morphé):* Our English word, "metamorphosis," comes from *morphé*. We use it to explain that while a caterpillar may change form to become a butterfly, its true nature remains the same. It literally means an outward expression of an inmost nature. For example, take the statement "The winning tennis player's form was excellent." Here, "form" would refer to the outward expression of inward ability. Jesus Christ is the outward expression of the essential nature of God. We have no English word to convey this.

"God": The word "God" is not preceded by an article (like "the" or "a"), thus essential nature is being stressed. Rather than being the very nature of a god, Jesus Christ is the very essence of God Himself.

"Made...of no reputation" *(kenoó):* This English phrase is only one word in the Greek. If a general going into battle wants to disguise himself from the enemy, he will take off all of his insignia which identify him as a general and then put on the common garb. The process of taking off the insignia is the word *"kenoó,"* which is translated here as *"made of no reputation."* Therefore, Christ voluntarily set aside the free exercise of his divine attributes.

"Fashion" *(schéma):* The Greek word refers to the outward mode and expression of either of two natures which are embodied within one figure. Therefore, this term indicates that Christ had two natures (divine and human), but by becoming a man, only his human nature was given outward expression.

"Unto death": In the Greek, this literally refers to the process leading up to death.

Studying the original grammar of this passage clearly shows that:

1. Jesus Christ was the exact inner essence of God the Father and also the outward expression of God in human form (vs. 6).

2. Although Christ was fully God, He voluntarily set aside the free exercise of his divine attributes and expressed Himself in the likeness of men (vs. 7-8).

3. Christ willingly became submissive to the will of the Father in the events leading up to, and including, His death (vs. 8. See also John 10:17-18).

This is why Christ prayed to the Father. It was an act of submission to His will.

Now that you have an understanding of the Greek word *morphé,* hopefully you will better understand what Jesus meant when He said, *"I and my Father are one."* The following verses shed further light on Christ as the *morphé* of God:

> John 1:1,14: *"In the beginning was the Word, and the Word was with God, and the Word was God .... And the Word was made flesh."*

John 14:8-9: *"Philip saith unto him, Lord, shew us the Father, and it sufficeth us. Jesus saith unto him, Have I been so long time with you, and yet hast thou not known me, Philip? He that hath seen me hath seen the Father; and how sayest thou then, shew us the Father?"*

Colossians 2:9: *"For in Him dwelleth all the fullness of the Godhead bodily."*

I Timothy 3:16: *"God was manifest in the flesh."*

WHY IT IS IMPORTANT TO BELIEVE IN THE TRUE IDENTITY OF JESUS CHRIST

Those who do not believe who Christ truly is will not have eternal life.

John 3:18, 36: *"He that believeth on him is not condemned: But he that believeth not is condemned already, because he hath not believed in the name of the only begotten Son of God...He that believeth on the Son hath everlasting life: and he that believeth not the Son shall not see life; but the wrath of God abideth on him."*

When the Bible talks of *"believing in the name"* of Christ, it is speaking of believing in His identity. *"Name of God"* is an Old Testament expression which refers to all that God is in His majesty, glory and power. In New Testament Greek, the phrase *"believing in the name"* of Christ includes all that He is in His glorious Person: His character, authority, majesty and power. Christ is

God. Therefore, believing in His *"name"* means to believe that Christ is God. We cannot become children of God unless we *"believe on His name"* (John 1:12).

> John 8:24: *"I said therefore unto you, that ye shall die in your sins: for if ye believe not that I am he, ye shall die in your sins."*

Only those who do believe in the true Christ will have eternal life.

> I John 5:12-13: *"He that hath the Son hath life; and he that hath not the Son of God hath not life. These things have I written unto you that believe on the name of the Son of God; that ye may know that ye have eternal life, and that ye may believe on the name of the Son of God."*

> John 17:3: *"And this is life eternal, that they might know thee the only true God, and Jesus Christ whom thou has sent."*

Challenge your friend to believe in the true Jesus of the Bible and submit to His true gospel of salvation (as outlined in the beginning of Chapter 8)!

Chapter Five

Exposing Mormonism's Other Gospel

Your Mormon friend does not know that the gospel of Mormonism is different than the gospel of the Bible. This chapter will assist you in sharing the true gospel with him. You can expose the LDS gospel as false in a step-by-step dialogue with your friend, then you will be able to challenge him to accept the true gospel.

Be sure your Mormon friend understands exactly what the LDS gospel is.

The LDS gospel is laws and ordinances for salvation:

> "We believe that through the Atonement of Christ, all mankind may be saved, by obedience to the laws and ordinances of the Gospel." (LDS third Article of Faith).

> "The gospel of Jesus Christ is the plan of salvation. It embraces all of the laws, principles, doctrines, rites, ordinances, acts, powers, authorities, and keys necessary to save and exalt men in the highest heaven hereafter..." (*Mormon Doctrine,* p. 331).

ASK: According to these statements, does the gospel have laws and ordinances? (Yes.)

What is the purpose of obeying the laws of this gospel? ("to save and exalt men in the highest heaven hereafter.")

What does it mean to "exalt men?" (Godhood.)

The LDS gospel teaches that men can become Gods.

Look at the definition given in *Gospel Principles*, pp. 289-290:

> "WHAT IS EXALTATION? Exaltation is eternal life, the kind of life that God lives. He lives in great glory. He is perfect. He possesses all knowledge and all wisdom. He is the father of spirit children. He is a creator. We can become Gods like our Heavenly Father. This is exaltation. If we prove faithful and obedient to all the commandments of the Lord, we will live in the highest degree of the celestial kingdom of Heaven. We will become exalted, just like our Heavenly Father."

ASK: Is it your goal to become a God just like your Heavenly Father? (This *is* the goal of Mormonism.)

Do you know what God says in the Bible about becoming a God?

> Isaiah 43:10: *"...before me there was no God formed, neither shall there be after me."*

According to God, men cannot become Gods.

Various LDS claims of men becoming Gods.

CLAIM #1: This verse is referring to idols, not true Gods.

YOUR RESPONSE: That is correct. It is because people were worshipping idol-gods that God reaffirms His position as the only true God (Isa. 44:9-20). Therefore, no true God has ever existed before Him or ever will exist after Him (43:10).

CLAIM #2: Jesus said, *"Be ye therefore perfect, even as your Father which is in heaven is perfect."* (Matt. 5:48).

YOUR RESPONSE: Jesus did not say to be a perfect God, but to have perfect character as God has. Read this verse in its context: Jesus said to turn the other cheek (vs. 39), give to others (vs. 40-42), and love your enemies (vs. 44,46). Therefore, be perfect (vs. 48). We are to strive for perfection in Godlike character. Nowhere in the Bible are we told to strive to become Gods.

CLAIM #3: Romans 8:17 says, *"And if children, then heirs; heirs of God, and joint-heirs with Christ; if so be that we suffer with him, that we may be also glorified together."* This means that we, like Christ, can inherit Godhood.

YOUR RESPONSE: First of all, Jesus never had to be an heir of Godhood. He is and always has been God. (John 1:1, Psalm 90:2).

Secondly, according to Romans 8, heirs are believers in Christ who inherit a position as children of God (vs. 14-16. Also John 1:12, Gal. 4:7).

Believers will also inherit His spiritual blessings (Eph. 1:3) and later, His glory in heaven (John 17:24; I Cor. 3:21 - 23). They will suffer (Col. 1:24; II Tim. 3:12) and share in Christ's glory (II Tim. 2:12; I Peter 4:13; 5:10).

CLAIM #4: Jesus said, *"Ye are gods"* (John 10:34).

YOUR RESPONSE: John 10:34 is a quotation of Psalm 82:6 where human judges were called gods, although they were merely men and would *"die like men."* Jesus was not telling these Jewish men that they were actual Gods. Nowhere in the Bible did He indicate that men can become Gods.

SHOW WHAT THE BIBLICAL GOSPEL IS

I Corinthians 15:1-5: *"Moreover, brethren, I declare unto you the **gospel** which I preached unto you, which also ye have received, and wherein ye stand; By which also ye are saved, if ye keep in memory what I preached unto you, unless ye have believed in vain. For I delivered unto you first of all that which I also received, how that Christ died for our sins according to the scriptures; And that he was buried, and that he rose again the third day according to the scriptures: And that he was seen of Cephas, then of the twelve..."*

Summarize what the gospel is:
1. Christ died for our sins (vs.3),
2. He was buried (vs. 4),
3. He rose again the third day (vs. 4),
4. He was seen by eyewitnesses (vs. 5-8).

The LDS Church claims that the gospel had been "lost to the earth" and was restored through Joseph Smith. However, it was never lost. Matthew, Mark, Luke and John each give an account of the gospel.

LDS CLAIM: The LDS Church does teach that Christ died and rose again.

YOUR RESPONSE: Yes, it does teach that Christ died and rose again. However, Mormonism teaches that the *gospel* is laws and ordinances which, if followed, will lead to Godhood.

Be sure your friend understands the differences between the two gospels.

The biblical gospel:	Christ died for our sins.
	Christ was buried.
	Christ was resurrected.
	Christ was seen.
The LDS gospel:	Man obeys laws.
	Man becomes a God.

Show the biblical warning about preaching "any other" gospel.

Galatians 1:8-9 *"But though we, or an angel from heaven, preach any other gospel unto you than that which we have preached unto you, let him be accursed. As we said before, so say I now again, if any man preach any other gospel unto you than that ye have received, let him be accursed."*

Can Mormonism be God's true church if it preaches any other gospel? (No!)

Summarize.

Encourage your Mormon friend to realize that Mormonism teaches a false gospel. It is not possible for men to become Gods. Explain why we need the true gospel as outlined in the beginning of Chapter 8.

Various LDS claims of salvation by works.

Mormons frequently challenge Christians with issues regarding salvation by works as opposed to salvation by grace through faith in Christ alone. For this reason, we need to be prepared for the most common LDS claims about salvation. You may not be challenged with all of these issues, but it will be helpful to have the responses available.

CLAIM #1: James chapter 2 teaches "salvation by works:" "*Even so faith, if it hath not works, is dead, being alone*" (vs. 17). "*Ye see then how that by works a man is justified, and not by faith only*" (vs. 24).

YOUR RESPONSE: Using the King James translation, it is easy to mistakenly interpret this passage to teach salvation by works. The problem is that the LDS Church does not study the New Testament in the original Greek language. The reason Christians know that James does not teach salvation by works is because the Greek grammar does not allow that interpretation. In James chapter 2, "*works*" does not refer to laws but instead to the evidence of our faith. "*Faith*" is a professed faith which produces no evidence that it exists.

CLAIM #2: John 14:15 says, "*If ye love me, keep my commandments.*"

YOUR RESPONSE: Does it say "keep my commandments to gain eternal life?" No. Christ simply said that we should keep His commandments if we love Him.

Do you agree with *Doctrine and Covenants* 1:31-32 where it states:

"For I the Lord cannot look upon sin
with the least degree of allowance; Never-
theless, he that repents and does the
commandments of the Lord shall be for-
given."

What happens if you miss a commandment? James
2:10 says, *"For whosoever shall keep the whole law,
and yet offend in one point, he is guilty of all."*

(Let him answer, then continue.)

Do you know what the Mormon prophet, Joseph F.
Smith, said about this verse (James 2:10)? In *Answers
to Gospel Questions*, vol. 3, page 26, he states:

"Therefore the words of James are true.
Unless a man can abide strictly in complete accord, he cannot enter there, and
in the words of James, he is guilty of all.
In other words if there is one divine law
that he does not keep he is barred from
participating in the kingdom."

According to the LDS gospel, you must obey the
whole law to obtain eternal life. This is impossible for
man (Isa. 64:6; Eccl. 7:20; Romans 3:10,23); that is
why it was necessary for Christ to provide salvation for
us.

CLAIM #3: Matthew 19:16-17 says, *"And, behold,
one came and said unto him, Good Master, what good
thing shall I do, that I may have eternal life? And he
said unto him, Why callest thou me good? There is none
good but one, that is, God: but if thou wilt enter into life,
keep the commandments."*

YOUR RESPONSE: Jesus answered the man's question truthfully. If you want to literally earn your way to eternal life, you must keep all the commandments (Lev. 18:5, James 2:10); but, this is impossible for men to do, as Jesus points out in His conclusion (vs. 26):

> "But Jesus beheld them, and said unto them, With men this is impossible; but with God all things are possible."

The Bible says that no man is perfect (Eccl.7:20, Rom. 3:10,23); that is why it was necessary for Christ to provide salvation for us (Rom. 5:8, I Pet. 3:18).

CLAIM #4: In Matthew 7:21, Jesus said, *"Not every one that saith unto me, Lord, Lord, shall enter into the kingdom of heaven; but he that doeth the will of my Father which is in heaven."*

YOUR RESPONSE: In the next verses, Jesus said, *"Many will say to me in that day, Lord, Lord, have we not prophesied in thy name? and in thy name have cast out devils? and in thy name done many wonderful works? And then will I profess unto them, I never knew you: depart from me, ye that work iniquity"* (vs. 22-23).

If doing many wonderful works is not the answer, then what does He mean when He said, *"He that doeth the will of my Father"* will enter into heaven? The answer is in John 6:40:

> "And this is the will of him that sent me, that every one which seeth the Son, and believeth on him, may have everlasting life: and I will raise him up at the last day." (Also see verses 28 and 29.)

The will of the Father is that you believe in Jesus Christ. (Challenge him to believe in the true identity of Christ discussed on p. 47.)

CLAIM #5: Revelation 20:13 says, "...and they were judged every man according to their works."

YOUR RESPONSE: This verse refers to the "great white throne" judgment mentioned in verse eleven. This judgment is only for those who never accepted Christ as their Savior. They will be judged according to their works. No believers will be at this judgment. Believers are already saved because they have received Christ (John 1:12; 3:16,18; I John 5:13). They are already written in the "book of life" (Rev. 3:5; 13:8; 17:8; 20:15; 21:27). Believers will be judged prior to the great white throne judgment, not for salvation, but to receive rewards (I Cor. 3:11-15; II Cor. 5:10; I Pet. 4:17-18).

If you do not receive the true Christ of the Bible as Savior, you will appear at the "great white throne" and be judged according to your works. On the basis of the following verses, do you want to be judged according to your works?

> Isaiah 64:6: "But we are all as an unclean thing, and all our righteousnesses are as filthy rags..."

> Romans 3:10, 20, 23: "As it is written, there is none righteous, no, not one.... Therefore by the deeds of the law there shall no flesh be justified in his sight...For all have sinned, and come short of the glory of God."

CLAIM #6: Do you mean we could just believe in Christ for an easy ticket into heaven?

YOUR RESPONSE: Believing in Christ is much more than an intellectual belief about Him. Even the demons believe and they tremble (James 2:19)! When the Bible urges us to *"believe"* in Christ for salvation, it uses the Greek word *"pisteuo"* which means *"to place trust and confidence in"* Him.

> *"That whosoever believeth (places trust and confidence) in him should not perish, but have eternal life"* (John 3:15).

We need to place our trust and confidence in Christ for salvation because we can never earn salvation by our own righteous acts (Rom. 3:10, 20, 23).

CLAIM #7: You say that salvation is not by works— it is by faith. But, faith is a work on our part.

YOUR RESPONSE: According to the Bible, faith is contrasted with works. Look at Ephesians 2:8-9:

> *"For by grace are ye saved through faith; and that not of yourselves: it is the gift of God: not of works, lest any man should boast."*

This verse states that we are *"saved through faith"* but *"not of works."* Therefore, faith is not a work. Faith is simply the hand that receives God's gracious gift of eternal life.

CLAIM #8: You say baptism is not necessary for salvation. Then why does the Bible speak of baptism for the dead, saying:

> *"Else what shall they do which are baptized for the dead, if the dead rise not at*

all? Why are they then baptized for the
dead?" (I Cor. 15:29).

(NOTE: Mormons believe that baptism is essential
for salvation. They also believe that we are given a
second chance to accept Mormonism as truth after we
die. Therefore, Mormons perform baptisms by proxy
for their dead relatives, hoping that they will accept
Mormonism as truth in the after-life. Mormons use
this verse in an attempt to convince us that Paul taught
baptism for the dead.)

YOUR RESPONSE: First of all, Paul referred to
"they," not *"we,"* who are baptized for the dead, thus
distinguishing the practice from his own. Paul merely
asked why those who deny that resurrection is possible
are baptizing for the dead at all.

The Bible does not teach that baptism is essential
for salvation. Biblically speaking, baptism follows the
salvation experience as a public testimony of our faith
(Acts. 10:47). Believers are, however, instructed to be
baptized, as we are instructed to do many things in the
Bible.

Not only is baptism for salvation unbiblical, but baptism for the dead implies a second chance for salvation
after death which is also unbiblical. (John 3:18,36; II
Thess. 1:8-9; Heb. 9:27).

CLAIM #9: In John 3:5, Jesus said, *"Except a man*
be born of water and of the Spirit, he cannot enter into
the kingdom of God." This means we must be baptized.

YOUR RESPONSE: First of all, baptism is not even
mentioned here. The term *"born of water"* most likely
refers to childbirth, as implied in the next verse:

*"That which is born of the flesh is flesh;
and that which is born of the Spirit is
spirit."*

Futhermore, the point Christ stressed is that we
must be born *"again"* (vs. 3 and 7). This second birth
is a spiritual birth necessary for salvation. In the early
church, believers were baptized after they had already
been saved and received the Holy Ghost (Acts 10:47).

CLAIM #10: Acts 2:38 tells us to be baptized *"for the
remission of sins."*

YOUR RESPONSE: The word translated *"for"* is the
Greek preposition *eis,* meaning *"because of"* the remission of our sins. In Matthew 12:41, *eis* is used in the
same way: *"They repented at (eis) the preaching of
Jonah."* Here, they repented *"because of"* his preaching, not "for the purpose of" his preaching. In Acts
2:38, the same applies: We are baptized *"because of"*
the remission of our sins.

Chapter Six

Exposing Joseph Smith as a False Prophet

If your friend's belief in Mormonism rests strongly on the premise that Joseph Smith was a true prophet, then it is possible to weaken his conviction by exposing Smith's false prophecies.

The test of a true prophet.

Challenge your friend with these questions:

How do you know that Joseph Smith was a true prophet? (His answer may be something like, "Because I have prayed about it." or "Because the Holy Ghost has testified to my heart that Joseph Smith was a true prophet.")

Do you know what the Bible says about how to determine if a prophet is true?

Read Deuteronomy 18:20-22 together:

> *"But the prophet, which shall presume to speak a word in my name, which I have not commanded him to speak, or that shall speak in the name of other gods, even that prophet shall die. And if thou say in thine heart, How shall we know the word which the LORD hath not spoken? When a prophet speaketh in the name of the LORD, if the thing follow not, nor come to pass, that is the thing which the LORD hath not spoken, but the prophet hath*

*spoken it presumptuously: thou shalt not
be afraid of him."*

Clarify the meaning of this passage:

If someone claims to be a prophet of God but his
prophecies fail to happen, he is a false prophet. According to the Bible, should we determine that Joseph
Smith was a true prophet by an inward testimony
about him or by verifying whether his prophecies came
true or not?

Read Jeremiah 23:32 together:

> *"Behold, I am against them that
> prophesy false dreams, saith the LORD,
> and do tell them, and cause my people to
> err by their lies, and by their lightness;
> yet I sent them not, nor commanded them:
> therefore they shall not profit this people
> at all, saith the LORD."*

Have you ever examined Joseph Smith's prophecies
to see if they came true?

False prophecies of Joseph Smith.

False prophecy #1: Christ would come by 1891.

ASK: Did you know that Joseph Smith prophesied
in 1835 that the coming of the Lord would be within
fifty-six years of that time?

(Give the following information to your friend and
ask him to verify it for himself:)

History of the Church, Volume 2, page 182, Kirk-
land, Ohio, February 14, 1835 reads:

"President Smith then stated that the meeting had been called, because God had commanded it; and it was made known to him by vision and by the Holy Spirit...the coming of the Lord, which was nigh—even fifty-six years should wind up the scene."

Did the Lord return in fifty-six years (1891)? Was this a true prophecy or a false prophecy?

False prophecy #2: A temple would be built in Missouri during Smith's generation.

ASK: Did you know that Joseph Smith prophesied falsely in *Doctrine and Covenants*? He prophesied that a temple would be built in Missouri during his generation.

Look in *Doctrine and Covenants* 84:

Verse 1: "A revelation of Jesus Christ unto his servant Joseph Smith, Jun..."

Verse 3: "Which city shall be built, beginning at the temple lot, which is appointed by the finger of the Lord, in the western boundaries of the State of Missouri..."

Verse 4: "Verily this is the word of the Lord, that the city New Jerusalem shall be built by the gathering of the saints, beginning at this place, even the place of the temple, which temple shall be reared in this generation."

Verse 5: "For verily this generation shall not all pass away until an house shall be built unto the Lord..."

Verse 31: "...which house shall be built unto the Lord in this generation, upon the consecrated spot as I have appointed."

Did you know that a temple was never built in Missouri during that generation or at any time after that? (NOTE: A generation is 110 years according to the *Book of Mormon*; 4 Nephi 18.) Was this a true prophecy or a false prophecy?

False prophecy #3: The people who were alive in 1833 would see the destruction of the wicked and the return of the lost tribes of Israel.

This prophecy is located in *History of the Church*, vol. 1, pp. 315-316. (Because many Mormons do not own a copy of this book, I have written it out for you below. Encourage your friend to obtain a copy of this book and look it up for himself at a later time.)

"And now I am prepared to say by the authority of Jesus Christ, that not many years shall pass away before the United States shall present such a scene of bloodshed as has not a parallel in the history of our nation; pestilence, hail, famine, and earthquake will sweep the wicked of this generation from off the face of the land, to open and prepare the way for the return of the lost tribes of Israel from the north country ... therefore I declare unto you the warning which the Lord has commanded to declare unto this generation.... Repent ye, repent ye, and embrace the everlasting covenant, and

flee to Zion, before the overflowing
scourge overtake you, for there are those
now living upon the earth whose eyes
shall not be closed in death until they see
all these things, which I have spoken, ful-
filled."

Didn't Joseph Smith prophesy that the people who
were alive in 1833 would see with their own eyes the
destruction of the wicked and the return of the lost
tribes of Israel? This never happened. Was this a true
prophecy or a false prophecy?

(Review with your Mormon friend what the Bible
says about false prophecy, and with that in mind, urge
him to seriously consider if Mormonism can actually
be true.)

Various LDS claims of biblical false prophecies.

Some Mormons have no problem with Joseph
Smith's false prophecies because they claim that there
are also biblical prophets who prophesied falsely—including Jesus Christ! This is not true, however, so we
must be prepared to refute their claims.

Following are some LDS claims of biblical false
prophecies, along with responses to those claims.
Remember this: there is not one false prophecy by a
biblical prophet of God. Each time you respond to a
claim of a biblical false prophecy, remind your Mormon
friend that a true prophet of God has never and can
never prophesy falsely—but Joseph Smith did!

CLAIM #1: Genesis 17:1-14 says circumcision was
to be an *"everlasting covenant,"* but the Apostle Paul
rejects circumcision in Romans 4 and Galatians 5.

YOUR RESPONSE: Paul did not reject circumcision —he merely pointed out that it was not necessary for salvation. Moreover, circumcision was not the covenant. The everlasting covenant was God's promise to give Abraham land and offspring (Chap. 15-16). That covenant is everlasting. Circumcision was merely a sign of that covenant, not the covenant itself (17:11).

CLAIM #2: Exodus 3:8-10 says that Moses was to lead Israel into the promised land, but he died before reaching the promised land.

YOUR RESPONSE: The Bible does not say that Moses would lead the Israelites into the promised land, rather, he would lead them out of Egypt (vs. 10). Furthermore, God proclaims in Numbers 20:12 that Moses would not bring them into the land.

CLAIM #3: Exodus 40:12-15; Numbers 25:10-13, say that the Aaronic Priesthood was to be "*everlasting*," but the Apostle Paul said the priesthood was changed (Heb. 7:12).

YOUR RESPONSE: The priesthood is everlasting, but not through the Aaronic order. During Old Testament times, the priesthood was through the Aaronic order but now it is through Christ because He is "*a priest for ever after the order of Melchizedec*" (Heb. 7:17). God's priesthood is still "*everlasting*" in Christ!

CLAIM #4: II Kings 20:1-6 says the prophet Isaiah promised Hezekiah that he would "*die and not live,*" but God added fifteen years to his life.

YOUR RESPONSE: Hezekiah died as Isaiah prophesied. This prophecy did not prohibit God from granting him an additional fifteen years.

CLAIM #5: Jeremiah 34:4-5 says that King Zedekiah would *"die in peace;"* but his eyes were put out, his children slaughtered and he died in a Babylonian prison (39:6-7).

YOUR RESPONSE: Zedekiah's peaceful death was conditional on his obedience to God. Because he was not obedient, he did not die in peace (Jer. 38:17,20; Ezek. 17:16).

CLAIM #6: Jonah 3:4 says that Nineveh *"shall be overthrown"* in forty days, but Nineveh was not overthrown.

YOUR RESPONSE: This prophecy was conditional on the people of Nineveh turning from their evil way. If they did, God would turn away from His anger (vs. 10).

CLAIM #7: Matthew 12:39-40 says that Christ's prediction of His resurrection after *"three days and three nights in the heart of the earth"* could not be true because He was crucified on Friday and resurrected only two days later on Sunday.

YOUR RESPONSE: The Jews counted part days as full days; they did not count days in twenty-four hour periods. Jesus was speaking to them with this in mind—if He died on Friday (the first day), then He would be resurrected on Sunday (the third day).

CLAIM #8: Matthew 24:34 says Christ prophesied that *"this generation shall not pass"* before His second coming, but He did not return during that generation.

YOUR RESPONSE: Christ was not talking about the generation of those living in New Testament times. In this context, Jesus was describing the end times (vs.

3-33). The term *"this generation"* refers to the generation that will be living during those times.

Chapter Seven

Dealing With Issues Your Mormon Friend Will Raise

I have never witnessed to a Mormon without being challenged by one or more of the issues covered in this chapter. Your friend will probably be very confident about discussing them. Do not feel intimidated by his confidence. Rather, stand firm in the boldness of our Lord, responding to his claims with a patient, loving attitude. It will be rewarding to be prepared for a discussion with your friend, knowing that there are biblical answers to each of his claims.

> "But in your hearts set apart Christ as Lord. Always be prepared to give an answer to everyone who asks you to give the reason for the hope that you have. But do this with gentleness and respect" (I Pet. 3:15 NIV).

Here are eight issues commonly raised by a Mormon, with responses to each claim:

1.   "I bear you my testimony that I know the Mormon Church is true and that Joseph Smith was a true prophet."

This is a "testimony" repeated almost word for word by Mormons throughout the world. You can hear it at LDS Church services every Sunday and spoken by Mormon missionaries to every potential convert. Your LDS friend may say it to you in an effort to convince you that Mormonism is God's true church.

YOUR RESPONSE: I, too, have a testimony. (Share your personal testimony of salvation through Christ.)

Personal testimonies are important but we cannot use them to determine God's truth. Truth must be based on what God says in His Word. God is the final authority over anyone's testimony. The Bible is *"profitable for doctrine, for reproof, for correction, for instruction in righteousness"* (II Tim. 3:16). If a testimony or belief is contrary to what God has already revealed to us in the Bible, then that testimony cannot be based on God's truth.

2. "Have you prayed to know if the Mormon Church is true?"

YOUR RESPONSE: Do you need to pray to know if Hinduism or the Bahai faith is true? Of course not. We know that neither of them can be God's true church because they both deny the truth of God's Word. The Bible tells us, *"Believe not every spirit, but try the spirits whether they are of God: because many false prophets are gone out into the world"* (I John 4:1). Mormonism cannot be God's true Church because it denies the truth of God's Word.

3. "We are Christians. We believe in Christ. The name of our church bears His name."

YOUR RESPONSE: There is one problem with that—you must first believe in the biblical identity of Christ to be a true Christian. (Share information in Chapter 4 about Christ.)

4. "Will you read the Book of Mormon?"

YOUR RESPONSE: I could, but did you know that the writer of the *Book of Mormon* excuses himself for not writing under the inspiration of God? He only *thinks* his writings are sacred and admits his tendency to err because of his own human weakness.

> I Nephi 19:6: "Nevertheless, I do not write anything upon plates save it be that I think it be sacred. And now, if I do err, even did they err of old; not that I would excuse myself because of other men, but because of the weakness which is in me, according to the flesh, I would excuse myself."

ALSO, on the first page, the *Book of Mormon* fails the LDS standard of being inspired by God:

The LDS Church claims that there can only be one prophet of God on earth at a time. However, on the first page of the *Book of Mormon* (I Nephi 1:4), the supposed prophet, Lehi, is said to have dwelt in Jerusalem during the first year of the reign of King Zedekiah. But according to the Bible, Jeremiah was the prophet in Jerusalem during that time (Jer. 1:1-3; 37:1-2). Therefore, Lehi could not have been a true prophet of God.

There is another problem with Lehi being a true prophet at that time in Jerusalem. Lehi prophesied that many inhabitants of Jerusalem would perish and that he and his family should depart from the Babylonian captivity (I Nephi 1:13-14; 2:2). But the Bible says this was the message of the false prophets. God said that none of the captives were to be free and they were to live and serve the king of Babylon in peace. The false prophets who claimed otherwise were the ones who would perish (Jer.27:6-17; 29:4-9)!

ALSO, the Book of Mormon contradicts God's first Word—the Bible. Alma 10:3 and Mosiah 2:3, in the

Book of Mormon state that descendants of Manasseh offered sacrifices according to the law of Moses. But the Bible is very clear that only the descendants of Aaron may give sacrifices at the altar (see Ex. 28:40-43; Num. 3:3-10; I Chron. 23:13; II Chron. 26:18; Heb. 7:12-14).

ASK: Since the *Book of Mormon* contradicts God's first Word, are you willing to believe that the *Book of Mormon* is from God?

ERRORS IN *DOCTRINE AND COVENANTS* REVEAL THAT IT ALSO IS A MAN-MADE WORK.

In section 76:100, Joseph Smith refers to Esaias and Isaiah as two different prophets, not realizing that Esaias is really the Greek name for Isaiah. A similar mistake can be found in *Doctrine and Covenants* 110:12-13. Apparently, Smith also did not know that Elias is the Greek name for Elijah.

ASK: Were these mistakes inspired by God or was this a man-made work?

5. "Why do you attack my church?"

YOUR RESPONSE: I'm not trying to attack your church; I just want you to be in heaven with me when we die. The LDS teachings about Christ and teachings about men becoming Gods are steering you away from true biblical salvation.

6. "Where do you get your authority?"

Mormons believe that Jesus conferred a priesthood authority upon the twelve apostles, who were then to pass it on to others. The Mormon Church teaches that after the apostles died, the priesthood authority was lost and God's true church was no longer on the earth. Joseph Smith claimed that John the Baptist came to earth in 1829 to ordain him to the Aaronic Priesthood. Later, Peter, James and John supposedly came and gave him the Melchizedec Priesthood.

This priesthood "authority" is very dear to Mormons. They believe this authority is necessary to perform all the LDS gospel ordinances for salvation. Since this is necessary from their perspective, they want to know where you get your authority to perform God's ordinances.

YOUR RESPONSE: I don't need any earthly priesthood for authority because all of the ordinances for salvation have been completed by Christ.

The Bible says that Christ *"sat down"* (Mark 16:19; Heb. 10:12). Ask any Jew what the phrase *"He sat down"* means. There were no chairs in the temple because the priests' work was never finished and they were therefore not allowed to sit down. Christ, however, sat down *"once for all"* (Heb. 10:10), having completed all work for salvation.

Those who receive Christ as Savior by believing in His *"name"* (His identity), receive complete authority, not to perform ordinances for salvation, but to become sons of God:

> *"But as many as received him, to them gave he power* [literally in Greek: "authority"] *to become the sons of God, even to them that believe on his name"* (John 1:12).

As sons of God, Christians have eternal life (John 3:16; I John 5:13) and are heirs of a holy and royal priesthood because they have placed their trust in Christ (See I Pet. 2:5-9; Rom. 8:14-17; Gal. 4:7).

(NOTE: The following information will help you understand the true biblical purpose of the Melchizedec and Aaronic priesthoods. I recommend sharing it with your friend after he has accepted Christ.)

According to the Bible, the Aaronic Priesthood could only be held by the descendants of Aaron who was of the tribe of Levi (See Ex. 28:40-43; Num. 3:3-10). Also, according to Hebrews chapter seven, the Aaronic Priesthood was *"annulled"* because it was *"weak and unprofitable."* Therefore, it was replaced by Christ, Who is our High Priest forever (Heb. 7:17-22; also Acts 13:39).

The Melchizedec Priesthood, according to Hebrews, is held only by Christ and cannot be passed on to anyone else. The Aaronic priests had to pass the priesthood from priest to priest because they eventually died. But Christ, because He *"continueth ever, hath an unchangeable priesthood"* (Heb. 7:24).

The word *"unchangeable"* does not mean that the priesthood itself does not change but rather that the priesthood does not change hands or transfer to someone else. The Greek word for *"unchangeable"* is *aparabatos* which literally means "that does not pass from one to another." Only Christ holds that priesthood!

If a Mormon were to hold the Melchizedec Priesthood, he would have to meet the biblical qualifications. Hebrews 7:16 says a Melchizedec priest has an *"endless life."* Verse 26 says he is *"holy ... separate from sinners, and made higher than the heavens."* He would have to be the One to "*offer up Himself*" for our sins and be "*consecrated for evermore*" (vs. 27-28).

7. "The Bible is incorrectly translated, full of errors and contradictions."

When a Mormon is confronted with a Bible verse that refutes Mormonism, he will often claim that the Bible is not accurate or that it contains errors. The LDS Church officially professes that the Bible is incorrectly translated:

> "We believe the Bible to be the word of God as far as it is translated correctly" (LDS eighth Article of Faith).

Mormons teach that the Bible has been corrupted through the centuries—that copyist mistakes have crept in and Scriptures have been lost. Therefore, they believe the Bible is not very reliable.

They couldn't be further from the truth! The LDS Church leaders have shut themselves off from the rest of the world in the precise science of textual criticism. Therefore, they are ignorant of the manuscript evidence from which our modern Bibles are translated. The Bible is universally accepted as the most accurate account of ancient history known to the world. Nothing compares with it! We can be assured that it is accurate, complete and correctly translated.

Responding to these issues is not a simple or short task. However, gaining general knowledge about the accuracy of the Bible will be a valuable asset when you share with your Mormon friend. The following is a basic overview to help you explain the reliability of the Bible. It is the same information which I wrote to Mormons in my booklet, *Speaking the Truth in Love.*

CONCERNING THE CLAIM OF BIBLICAL INAC-
CURACY:

The original writings, called "autographs," are no
longer in existence. How then, can we know that what
we have recorded in the Bible today is actually what
was originally written? How can we know that each
and every verse is accurate?

The original New Testament Scriptures were the
most frequently copied and widely circulated books in
history. In the first centuries A.D., thousands of copies
were written by different men in various countries and
cultures—all giving us the same account! There are
now more than 5,300 known Greek manuscripts. Add
over 10,000 Latin Vulgate and at least 9,300 other early
versions, and we have more than 24,000 manuscript
copies in existence today—some dated as early as A.D.
125! No other writing in history has been preserved
with such a wealth of authentification. The more
manuscripts available, the more agreement with the
original autographs is assured.

In addition to the manuscripts, we have quotations
of the Scriptures from the first century by the early
church fathers. All twenty-seven books of the New Testament were written, copied and begun to be dis-
tributed among the churches before the end of the first
century. Totaling over 36,000, the quotations of the
church fathers still exist and include the entire New
Testament except for eleven verses. The New Testament could virtually be reconstructed from them
without the use of manuscripts. We also have early
century lectionaries, non-biblical authors and first
century historians, each giving support to the accuracy
of the manuscripts.

The reliability of the Old Testament also is supported by overwhelming evidence. Thousands of ancient Hebrew manuscripts have been preserved through the centuries and can be seen in museums around the world. The Jewish Scriptures were copied in a highly formal manner with extreme care and reverence, resulting in an accurate text handed down throughout ancient history. The important discovery of the Dead Sea Scrolls in 1947 (dating back to the Third Century B.C.) confirms the accuracy of the Old Testament as it was written by Jewish scribes centuries before Christ.

CONCERNING THE CLAIM OF "VARIANT READINGS" IN THE MANUSCRIPT COPIES:

Mormons point out the fact that there are 150,000 places where variant readings or copyist mistakes occur in the manuscripts and conclude that the Bible cannot be trusted. However, these 150,000 "variant readings" are all variations in spelling and a small number of paraphrased renderings. None of the variations would in any way alter a single doctrine or meaning. Variant readings are not an issue at all.

CONCERNING THE CLAIM OF "MISSING SCRIPTURES:"

In an attempt to prove that God's truth is incomplete in the Bible, the LDS Church also claims that there are Scriptures missing from the Bible. They point to I Corinthians 5:9 where Paul says, *"I wrote unto you in an epistle..."* Also, they refer to some prophecies of Enoch quoted in Jude 1:14 which are not contained in any other area of Scripture.

The Bible does not say that these other writings are Scriptures. Just because the Bible refers to, or quotes from, another source does not mean that the other source was inspired. For example, Paul quotes a Cretian prophet in Titus 1:12, but this Cretian was not a prophet of God.

LDS Missionary reference books teach that there is another epistle to the Ephesians which is missing. They quote Ephesians 3:3 where Paul states, *"As I wrote afore in few words,"* and conclude that this refers to an earlier epistle. However, it does not. According to the text, Paul is reminding his readers that he has written about a mystery (defined in v.6) *"afore in few words"* in the previous chapters (1:3-14; 2:12,16,19). Paul also discusses this mystery in his earlier epistle to the Galatians.

To say that there are Scriptures missing is to claim that Christ lied when He said, *"Till heaven and earth pass, one jot or one tittle shall in no wise pass from the law, till all be fullfilled"* (Matt. 5:18). Isaiah assured us:

> *"The grass withereth, the flower fadeth:*
> *but the word of our God shall stand for*
> *ever"* (Isa. 40:8).

CONCERNING THE CLAIM THAT THE BIBLE IS "INCORRECTLY TRANSLATED:"

The LDS eighth Article of Faith states, "We believe the Bible to be the word of God as far as it is translated correctly ... "but the LDS Church does not present what they feel to be a more correct translation.

The Christian Church, however, is not dependent on modern translations for biblical accuracy. We can study directly from the original languages.

The New Testament was written in the *koiné* Greek which was the universal language from 330 B.C. to A.D. 330. This language was used and understood throughout the civilized world—it was spoken as freely on the streets of Rome, Alexandria and Jerusalem as in Athens. The construction and grammar of this language are understood completely, not only in the New Testament, but also in existing literary *koiné*, private letters, contracts, wills, government documents, etc. The *koiné* Greek, in which our New Testament was written, was the ordinary language of the people. The language is precise and clearly understandable. It is through the *koiné* Greek text that we can know exactly what the Bible teaches!

Because Mormons have not chosen to study the Bible in the original languages, they are missing out on the excitement of digging deeply into God's Word. Each phrase in the Bible can be translated with precision through proper study, giving us an understanding of the exact meaning of words within their context. There is so much biblical truth to study in the original languages and yet the Latter-day Saints do not take advantage of the opportunity. Because of this, they are unaware of God's true message of salvation.

CONCERNING THE CLAIM OF CONTRADICTIONS IN THE BIBLE:

When a Mormon says that there are contradictions in the Bible, we can simply say, "Really? Could you show me just one?" Here are the two most common LDS claims of biblical contradictions:

Mormons claim that there is a contradiction between two accounts of the same incident in the book of Acts:

ACTS 9:7—"And the men which journeyed with him stood speechless, hearing a voice, but seeing no man."

ACTS 22:9—"And they that were with me saw indeed the light, and were afraid; but they heard not the voice of him that spake to me."

They believe that there is a contradiction between "hearing a voice" in Acts 9 and "heard not the voice" in Acts 22. In Acts 9, the Greek verb "hearing" (akouo) is used with the noun "voice" in the genitive case, expressing sound being heard. In Acts 22, it is used with the noun in the accusative case, describing mental apprehension and simply declares that they did not understand. The men heard the sound of the voice but they did not understand it. There is no contradiction.

Mormons also claim that there is a contradiction between two accounts of Judas' death:

MATTHEW 27:5: "And he cast down the pieces of silver in the temple, and departed, and went and hanged himself."

ACTS 1:18: "...and falling headlong, he burst asunder in the midst, and all his bowels gushed out."

This is not a contradiction, but rather two aspects of Judas' death. He could have "fallen headlong" from the tree in which he hung himself.

8.   "All this talk about what the Bible says in Greek—are you a Greek scholar?"

It is not necessary to personally understand *koiné* Greek. The Greek text of the Bible, its literal translation and Greek word studies are available at any Christian bookstore. The *koiné* Greek is not a lost language. Any Greek scholar, regardless of his own religious beliefs, can tell us what the Greek text literally says. Anyone can obtain this information and read it for himself.

Chapter Eight

Leading Your Friend to Christ

It is my prayer that your Mormon friend will accept the truth about Christ and desire to receive Him as Lord and Savior. This chapter was written to help you clarify to your friend what he must understand about becoming a Christian.

1. **Because of sin:**
   a. We are separated from God.

   Isaiah 59:2: *"But your iniquities have separated you from your God; your sins have hidden his face from you, so that he will not hear."*

   b. Our righteousness falls short of God's standard.

   Isaiah 64:6: *"All of us have become like one who is unclean, and all our righteous acts are like filthy rags..."*

   Ecclesiastes 7:20: *"There is not a righteous man on earth who does what is right and never sins."*

   Romans 3:10,23: *"As it is written: There is no one righteous, not even one .. for all have sinned and fall short of the glory of God."*

   c. We cannot enter into the kingdom of Heaven by our own righteousness.

   Matthew 5:20: *"For I tell you that unless your righteousness surpasses that of the Pharisees and the teachers of the law, you will certainly not enter the kingdom of heaven."*

2. Because God is loving and merciful, He sent Jesus Christ to pay the penalty for our sins.

Romans 5:8: *"But God demonstrates his own love for us in this: While we were still sinners, Christ died for us."*

Romans 6:23: *"For the wages of sin is death, but the gift of God is eternal life in Christ Jesus our Lord."*

II Corinthians 5:19,21: *"God was reconciling the world to himself in Christ, not counting men's sins against them...God made him who had no sin to be sin for us, so that in him we might become the righteousness of God."*

The whole Bible is about one great transaction which Christ performed on our behalf—that is the "gospel" of Jesus Christ. By His death and resurrection, He paid for our sins and provided the only way for us to come to God:

I Peter 3:18: *"For Christ died for sins once for all, the righteous for the unrighteous, to bring you to God..."*

3. Christ's payment for our sins is available only to those who personally trust Him as Lord and Savior.

a. Those who do not place their trust in Christ will not go to Heaven:

II Thessalonians 1:8-9: *"He will punish those who do not know God and do not obey [submit to] the gospel of our Lord*

Jesus. They will be punished with ever-lasting destruction and shut out from the presence of the Lord and from the majes-ty of his power."

John 3:36: *"...Whoever rejects the Son will not see life, for God's wrath remains on him."*

b. Those who place their trust in Christ will have eternal life.

John 1:12: *"Yet to all who received him, to those who believed in his name, he gave the right to become children of God."*

John 3:16: *"For God so loved the world that he gave his one and only Son, that whoever believes in him shall not perish but have eternal life."*

Leading your friend in prayer:

Once your friend understands his need for Christ and desires to accept Him as his Lord and Savior, ask if you may lead him in prayer:

"Dear Lord Jesus,

I know that I am a sinner, separated from God. I believe that You died for my sins. I want to trust in You as Lord and Savior. Lord, forgive my sin and come into my life. Thank You for Your gracious gift of eternal life.

In Jesus' name, Amen."

What to share immediately with your new Christian friend:

Through Christ, God completely forgives your sins.

> Romans 10:13: *"Everyone who calls on the name of the Lord will be saved."*

> Hebrews 8:12: *"For I will forgive their wickedness and will remember their sins no more."*

You have the assurance of eternal life.

> I John 5:13: *"I write these things to you who believe in the name of the Son of God so that you may know that you have eternal life."*

The Spirit of Christ lives in you.

> Galatians 2:20: *"I have been crucified with Christ and I no longer live, but Christ lives in me. The life I live in the body, I live by faith in the Son of God, who loved me and gave himself for me."*

> I Corinthians 6:19: *"Do you not know that your body is a temple of the Holy Spirit, who is in you, whom you have received from God?..."*

> Hebrews 13:5: *"...God has said, 'Never will I leave you; never will I forsake you.'"*

Your testimony can now be based on the promises of God's Word, instead of on your feelings. Good feelings come and go, but the facts of God's Word and the promise of eternal life remain true and consistent.

How to grow as a Christian.

Focus on Christ every day!

> Colossians 2:6-7: *"So then, just as you received Christ Jesus as Lord, continue to live in him, rooted and built up in him, strengthened in the faith as you were taught, and overflowing with thankfulness."*

> Proverbs 3:5-6: *"Trust in the LORD with all your heart and lean not on your own understanding; in all your ways acknowledge him, and he will make your paths straight."*

Pray every day!

> Philippians 4:6-7: *"Do not be anxious about anything, but in everything, by prayer and petition, with thanksgiving, present your requests to God. And the peace of God, which transcends all understanding, will guard your hearts and your minds in Christ Jesus."*

Read from the Bible every day!

> II Timothy 3:16-17 *"All Scripture is God-breathed and is useful for teaching, rebuking, correcting and training in righteousness, so that the man of God may be thoroughly equipped for every good work."*

Be baptized as a testimony of your faith.

> Matthew 28:19: *"Therefore go and make disciples of all nations, baptizing*

them in the name of the Father and of the Son and of the Holy Spirit."

Acts 2:41: *"Those who accepted his message were baptized..."*

Fellowship with other Christians regularly.

Hebrews 10:24-25: *"And let us consider how we may spur one another on toward love and good deeds. Let us not give up meeting together, as some are in the habit of doing, but let us encourage one another—and all the more as you see the Day approaching."*

Tell others about Christ.

I Peter 3:15: *"But in your hearts set apart Christ as Lord. Always be prepared to give an answer to everyone who asks you to give the reason for the hope that you have. But do this with gentleness and respect."*

In closing

As a more mature Christian, you now have the exciting responsibility to help your friend learn more about his new relationship with Christ. Matthew 28:19-20 tells us not only to *"make disciples of all nations"* but to *"teach them."* Be sure to maintain close contact, helping him to *"grow in the grace and knowledge of our Lord and Savior Jesus Christ"* (II Pet. 3:18).

INDEX OF SUBJECTS

INDEX OF BIBLE QUOTATIONS

BIBLIOGRAPHY

Hocking, David L. *The Nature of God in Plain Language.*
Word Books, 1984.

McDowell, Josh. *Evidence That Demands a Verdict.*
Here's Life Publishers, 1972, 1979.

McKeever, Bill. *Answering Mormons' Questions.*
Mormon Research Ministry, 1987.

Morey, Robert A. *How to Answer a Mormon.*
Bethany House Publishers, 1983.

Ryrie, Charles C. *Basic Theology.*
Victor Books, 1987.

Spencer, James R. *Have You Witnessed to a Mormon Lately?*
Chosen Books, 1986.

Tope, Wally. *On the Frontlines.* 1980

Walvoord, John F. and Roy B. Zuck. *The Bible Knowledge Commentary* (two volumes). Victor Books, 1985.

GREEK EXPOSITION

Archer, Gleason L. *Encyclopedia of Bible Difficulties.* Zondervan Publishing House, 1982.

Dana Th.D., H.E. and Julius R. Mantey, Th.D., D.D. *A Manual Grammar of the Greek New Testament.* MacMillan Co., 1929.

Vine, W.E. *The Expanded Vine's Expository Dictionary of New Testament Words.* Bethany House Publishers, 1984.

Wuest, Kenneth S. *Word Studies from the Greek New Testament.* III vols. Wm. B. Eerdmans Publishing Co., 1973.